The Walls
of
My Heart

Mary Hale

www.WeAreAPS.com

ISBN: 978-1-945145-48-3

APS Publishing
2653 S. Lawndale
Chicago, IL 60623
847-942-6135
www.WeAreAPS.com

Table of Contents

Part 1

The Red Heart: Brokenness

Introduction

Everyone has a story to tell; it is called our history. It consists of our happy and sad times. We also have times when we feel alone and devastated by things that have happened or were spoken to us, whether past or present.

We allow those things that have devastated us to follow us through life and begin to act on them and build a brick wall as a shield of protection. We never allow ourselves to heal from the past, so we carry those bricks around with us. They not only affect us personally, but our loved ones and those that we meet as well. For out of the heart flows the issues of life.

Let the Healing Begin

We all know that a castle was primarily used for war as a means of protection. The castle was originally built by laying a foundation of cement, and it was layered with bricks, which turned into walls. Did you know that in life we also build castle walls?

In a vision, I saw myself walking through a garden. The garden was dark and gloomy as if it had no life and was deserted. There was a pedway that took me through the garden of wilted flowers. As I looked from a distance, I saw a castle that looked like it had been abandoned. As I got closer, there were tall trees covering something. I could see that it was dark and gloomy; there was no light. It was as if no one lived in the castle.

As I began to approach the castle behind the trees, I saw a large red heart standing in front of the castle. It was almost as tall as the castle, but it had been hidden by the trees. The heart had a crack in the middle. It had a flow of blood running out of it slowly, and it was swollen. I had a lot of questions running through my head. I thought to myself, "Why is a broken heart in front of a castle? Why was it red, yet the castle had no color"? I never gave a thought that this might not be a place to enter because I felt so comfortable being in this place.

I walked past the heart toward the castle. The castle was about a block away. I avoided getting blood on my shoes because I somehow went around the heart. As I was walking,

I could not get over the fact that the heart was that big. But, why was the heart cracked and bleeding? Who would put a heart in front of a castle? What did the heart represent? There were a series of questions I had going on in my head, but all I could do was look at the heart from a distance as I was walking.

Once I turned, I saw that the castle was now about a half block away from the heart. When I arrived, I entered the castle. It had no doors inside, just tall ceilings and walls, and it was made of bricks. There were no furnishings or pictures; it looked dusty and empty with cobwebs. It was so cold and dark. It looked as if it had been empty for a long time. There was a balcony leading upstairs. There were stairs on both sides of the entry with no windows.

There were about 15 stairs on each side of the balcony. As I went up the stairs, I entered the second floor of the castle. There were about five or six empty rooms, but no doors or windows. This castle was empty. It looked as if no one ever lived in it. Straight ahead was another set of stairs that led to a large room with no windows – just a brick wall. I thought to myself, "This must have been a hiding place". I went back downstairs and noticed that there was no other entrance or exit aside from where the red heart was located. So, I went outside the castle and looked around.

There was no way around the castle. The bricks would not allow me to pass, so I went back into the castle. As I entered, I noticed an open room under the stairs. This opening led to another large room, which had a window, however, I was unable to open it. It was a large glass sealed by the bricks.

I looked out the window and saw a

beautiful garden with a lot of colorful flowers. There was another heart in the garden that was gold. It was not as large as the red heart, and it was glowing and beautiful. I stood amazed at the heart and tried to understand why the red heart was blocking castle, yet the gold heart was in the back of the castle. I really didn't understand what was going on, so I went back upstairs.

In my vision, I gave no thought to what was happening. Instead, I began to label and assign each room, which seemed to represent my life and feelings about the incidents that occurred as far as relationships with family, friends, co-workers, and others who affected my life. I even categorized each room for every person that was part of my life in the past as well as the present. I assigned each person to a room by labeling their name to the walls of the corresponding rooms.

They were assigned to a room according to where I allowed them to enter. I did not assign them to the room where I thought they would be comfortable because it was my room and my castle. I placed them in the rooms in which I wanted them. These rooms were labeled Hate, Heartache, Disappointment, Pain, and Rejection. The only good room in the castle was underneath the stairs with the window by the gold heart, which was the one place I was unable to enter.

I was on my way downstairs and heard laughter, but I knew there was no one in the castle but me. I went to the room under the stairs and looked out of the window into the courtyard. There was the gold heart shining and sparkling with my children and grandchildren standing right next to it. They were talking, laughing, and enjoying life. I could tell they loved being close to that heart.

I sat in the room under the stairs

looking out at the window of opportunity, but not able to open it. I wondered why they were in the yard, yet I couldn't get to them? I could not find an entry into the garden. There was no door, and I couldn't open the window because it was sealed with bricks. I could not enter the courtyard. I could only see them being happy and enjoying the heart.

Suddenly, it was quiet. I could see them but could no longer hear the laughter. The heart was pumping quite fast; it was happy and excited. No one else including me could enter the courtyard – only the ones that I saw through the window. It was then that I realized that the red and gold hearts were mine, and the castle I was in was the walls of the foundation that I had built. These were the bricks that I'd laid for many years, which explained why there were spider webs and darkness. These were the bricks that had held me captive for so long regarding my life and the people therein.

These brick walls resulted from things that had been spoken over my life as well as my experiences. As we get older, if we never allow closure to occur, the walls will affect who we ultimately become – whether positive or negative. The ridiculous thing about it is that we allow the negative force to build and become a jail, not a protective force but a jail. We are prisoners in our own mind. The problem is once the wound is put in place, it leaves scar tissue and healing never takes place, which means our destiny is altered all because of what happened in the past.

The only person holding us captive is ourselves. Why? Because we have built this castle full of rejection, which destroys self-esteem. Now, we live with regret and sorrow because somewhere in our lives someone said, "You will never be anything"; "You are ugly"; "You're skinny"; "You are fat"; "You're stupid", etc. These statements made us feel as if no one cared and so we built the walls of defense because we felt defeated, which caused us to defend ourselves against any and everything. Then, the enemy of abandonment, self-pity, hatred, insecurity, worthlessness, unforgiveness, and envy manifests. These are the bricks that build through life and we reside within these walls of emotional scars. Once these walls are built, there are no windows, doors, or circulation. We are trapped, and we die in the castle.

I built these brick walls and they became empty rooms with no doors or furnishings – absolutely nothing inside but emptiness. These empty walls created a castle because I never took the time to deal with the red broken heart on the outside of the castle. I knew then that the red heart represented heartache, disappointment, and pain from the past I experienced but never resolved. I never tried to forgive or repair the things that happened to me in the past.

Let the Journaling Begin…

List some emotions that you are holding on to that you feel may be keeping you from your destiny.

_____

_____

_____

_____

_____

_____

_____

_____

_____

_____

_____

_____

_____

_____

_____

_____

_____

_____

_____

_____

Name the people that you need to forgive, or individuals with which you have unresolved issues.

_____

_____

_____

_____

_____

_____

_____

_____

_____

_____

_____

_____

_____

_____

_____

_____

_____

_____

_____

_____

_____

Past or present, list some incidents that you believe may be responsible for you creating brick walls.

_____

_____

_____

_____

_____

_____

_____

_____

_____

_____

_____

_____

_____

_____

_____

_____

_____

_____

_____

_____

What are some things you may be
able to do to provide yourself closure?

_____

_____

_____

_____

_____

_____

_____

_____

_____

_____

_____

_____

_____

_____

_____

_____

_____

_____

_____

_____

_____

_____

_____

Part 2

The Gold Heart: Restoration

Self-Reflection

The gold heart represented the future, or my destiny. In my vision, I was pleading with myself – trying to figure out how I could open the window with the gold heart. The window was sealed with bricks so that I could not continue to build another castle because of generational curses.

How can I get to my future if I don't resolve the issues of my past? I realized I am stuck. I am in a castle of protected walls. There are no doors for closure of the past; there is only one window.

I said to myself, "These are not new walls. These walls are made of stony bricks and have been building for a long time because now they are walls that have accumulated from the first brick that was laid. This built the foundation and strengthened me to build this castle. A habitation of brick and mortar and tar.

Walls are structured bricks or stones that surround an area or separate one area from another. A structure is the way something was built or arranged or organized. When I built each structure, it became a wall and closed everything and everybody out.

There were no doors because I never had closure. I'd held all these bricks in my heart and it got too heavy, so the heart overloaded, swelled and cracked. Situations and circumstances, setbacks and turnarounds in my life caused me to build bricks that turned into walls. These bricks were built from my mother's womb because they carried things that had been said and done to her while she was carrying me. Things that had been spoken over my life from childhood to adolescence to my teen years, and now as an adult.

The heart is red. It pumps blood. Without it, there is no life. If the heart is losing its resources, it dies and becomes as stony as the castle.

I have lived my life through a protected wall with no closure.

The heart was never able to enter the castle because it was so damaged and swollen. There was no real love or joy. The heart is important, but if it is broken, it must be healed. Otherwise, it is losing its ability to love. It is bleeding out, but nothing good is going in. The only thing that enters is bitterness and rejection and other negative feelings.

The heart is associated with red, and red is associated with life, romance, passion, joy, and excitement. It has a lot to do with our emotions – the way we feel and think; our social, spiritual, and physical well-being. We all have a desire to be held, loved, and needed whether from family, friends, lovers, etc. This desire starts from the mother's womb.

The heart that was in front of the castle was cracked and damaged. It was my heart. I had been suffering in my soul and didn't know any better. When we are in denial, we suffer. I want to repair my heart so that the castle will have doors to each room. I want to be able to open the window to the heart of gold.

When I realized this was my desire, I made the decision to go back to the red heart in front of the castle where it all began because the heart represented love and security; the ability to care for other people unconditionally with an understanding of their need for love as well as my own. Bitterness and rejection caused the heart to crack.

I went back to the front of the castle where the heart was located. But in order to get to the heart, I had to step into the blood and allow the healing to begin. When I stepped into the blood, there was an instant change, and as I began to walk the pavement toward the castle, it began to change colors. It was no longer pale and dingy looking.

I began to walk a little further. As I began to walk faster, I felt free and as I was walking, I could see there were red roses surrounding the castle. The grass was greener, and I could see the castle walls were no longer dark gray. Things began to come alive in the castle and alive in me – physically, mentally, spiritually, emotionally, and financially.

When I returned to the castle, I noticed all the labels I'd assigned to each room had began to fall off. Each room that represented my life now had new meaning from what I'd previously felt. I had a new outlook on my past life experiences. The healing had begun. I no longer wanted to categorize each room for every person that was part of my life in the past or present. This was a new beginning.

I realized this was my castle, my wall of protection, and whatever I do in life will affect my life. I opened the window of love, joy, and peace. So now, I could enter the courtyard and be with the gold heart.

"A new heart also will I give you, and a new spirit will I put within you: and I will take away the stony heart out of your flesh, and I will give you an heart of flesh. And I will put my spirit within you, and cause you to walk in my statutes, and ye shall keep my judgments, and do them."

**Ezekiel 36:26, 27
(King James Version)**

Let the Journaling Continue...

What does your future look like once you have forgiven those that hurt you?

_____

_____

_____

_____

_____

_____

_____

_____

_____

_____

_____

_____

_____

_____

_____

_____

_____

_____

_____

_____

_____

What does your future look like once you have forgiven yourself?

_____

_____

_____

_____

_____

_____

_____

_____

_____

_____

_____

_____

_____

_____

_____

_____

_____

_____

_____

_____

_____

Part 3

Making the Transition

Changing for the Better

When we live in an altered state, as human beings, we put ourselves above the reality of what is truly happening in our lives and we do not want to deal with it. We make the mistake of building false pride. The Bible says that the heart, the conscience of man, in his corrupt and fallen state is deceitful.

The deceitfulness of the heart cheats us when we are led by our own understanding and it will ruin us and bring us to a place of heartache, despair, low self-esteem, and wickedness.

Wicked is a strong word and very sinful. The word wicked means, "a mental disregard for justice, righteousness, truth, honor, virtue; evil in thought and life; depravity; sinfulness; criminality."

Sometimes we are not aware of the wickedness in our heart, but it does exist; to what extent, only God knows. We are deceived and destroyed by our own delusional thoughts. Who can know how bad our own heart is, let alone the hearts of others? But God sees the wickedness and knows it because He searches the heart. God knows our intent, what is concealed, and what is disguised in it.

The heart has an emotional function. It controls the will and emotions. Rejection, betrayal, and abandonment will put you in a place of darkness. Rejection is very powerful. It plays a big part in our lives especially when we are in denial. Rejection is "the denial of a person's affection; not receiving them; not allowing something."

The heart reacts when we are at peace,

when we are troubled, when we rejoice, when we love and when we fear. The heart affects us in so many ways mentally and physically. It plans, makes commitments, and decides. The heart controls what our final answer will be and how we will react.

However, it can never be said that the heart is unable to change. It can...I am a living witness. I have been in denial for a long time. It is like not taking the medicine that has been prescribed for you because you don't think you are sick. Although, I have learned that physical pain and rejection can affect us in the same way – the heartache simply has more to do with our emotions.

So, I speak to your heart as well as my own. Allow your heart to mend. My castle of protection is still present, but now I can begin to repair it so that it has life and is no longer dark and gloomy. The healing has begun.

Other Books by Mary Hale:

Emotional Baggage
The Formation of My Walls
The Castle of My Heart

Interested in having your
book published?
Contact APS Publishing

APS Books & More
2653 S. Lawndale
Chicago, IL 60623
847-942-6135
www.WeAreAPS.com